"center of everything," seems most appropriate as the city is truly the heart of the country to which everything is drawn. It is the hub of transportation, commerce, government, education and culture and home to over 20 percent of the nation's population.

Seoul is often, and most appropriately, called a "city of contrasts." It is both ancient and modern, steeped in tradition yet full of vitality, a harmonizing of the old and the new. It sparkles with the glass and steel of modern high-rise hotels, office complexes and shopping centers but the quaintness and charm of another era can still be found in the areas they overshadow. Most of Seoul's modern facade has been constructed in the past 30 years as the city was virtually destroyed during the fratricidal Korean War of 1950-53; miraculously, and most fortunate for everyone, many of its ancient structures survived.

There are many things to see and do in Seoul and its vicinity. Besides excellent hotels, nightclubs, casinos, and an array of restaurants serving a variety of cuisines, the downtown

The main artery is the Han River, and on its banks is the pulsating heart of the country, Seoul. Along the Han, there is a park where the citizens take a walk in the sunshine and play ball.

offers gardens, palaces, museums, parks, galleries, and theaters as well as traditional markets, modern department stores and numerous underground shopping arcades where some of the best buys in the world can be found. A variety of archeological sites, ancient fortresses, royal tombs, religious hermitages, shrines, temples and potteries are located in the suburbs where golf courses and other sports facilities also abound. There are also a number of large parks with amusement and recreational facilities for the young, zoos and botanical gardens.

Shown here is part of the Olympic Taero, a 36-kilometer-long expressway along the Han River connecting the Kimpo International Airport with the Seoul Sports Complex that was opened May 2, 1986.

PALACES IN SEOUL

The large and small palaces that add color to the metropolitan cityscape are by far the most splendid of Seoul's tangible cultural heritage. To walk among their gardens is to travel back in time to when history was shaped and recorded beneath brilliantly decorated ceilings and under the watchful gaze of ornate clay figures perched on roof ridges to ward off evil.

Only four of the five palaces that were built during the Yi Dynasty remain: Kyŏngbokkung in the north; Ch'angdŏkkung and Ch'anggyŏnggung in the east; and Tŏksugung in the south. Fortunately, they are all conveniently located within a 30- or 40-minute walk of the downtown area.

Kwanghwamun Gate and the domed building, which was the symbol of the national government until it recently became the home of the National Museum, are two of the most famous landmarks in Seoul.

KYŎNGBOKKUNG

This, the "Palace of Shining Happiness," is at once the oldest and newest of Seoul's palaces as it was first built in 1395 and reconstructed in the mid-1800s. The home of kings and the principal site of royal audiences and other court functions until 1592, when it was destroyed during a Japanese invasion of Korea, it is now the home of the National Folklore Museum and a popular place for school outings.

Only part of the palace wall is intact and only a few of the structures, which originally numbered in the hundreds, remain as many were destroyed by fire and war and many were dismantled for the construction of other palaces. Many stone monuments and pagodas moved from other parts of the country are located on the palace grounds.

正七品

KŬNJŎNGJŎN AND KYŎNGHOERU

Kŭnjŏngjŏn, the main throne hall, faces south down the main axis of the city. It is said that Namdaemun (South Gate), which is 2.2 kilometers away, was visible from its throne. Stone fire-eating beasts called *haet'ae* stand at the steps and corners of the stone railings to protect the double-roofed hall from fire. To each side of the royal walkway leading to the throne is a row of inscribed stone tablets marking the position of the court and military officials, the highest rank being closest to the hall. Covered corridors encircle the flagstoned courtyard and house a collection of stone relics.

Kyŏnghoeru, which was used for receptions, festivals and state examinations, is still used for official government functions. The large pavilion standing in a lotus pond, is a monument to the skills and the aesthetic sensibilities of Korea's ancient architects.

Kŭnjŏngjŏn, the throne hall of Kyŏngbokkung Palace, and the place in its courtyard where officials stood during royal audiences (left).

Kyŏnghoeru, or the "Hall of Happy Meetings" (below) is one of the most photographed structures in Korea.

KYŎNGCH'ŎNSA PAGODA

Just inside the entrance to Kyŏngbokkung is one of Korea's most elaborate pagodas. It is believed to have been made in 1348 as a wedding present for a princess. Its name comes from an ancient temple near Kaesŏng (a city in North Korea) called Kyŏngch'ŏnsa where it was supposedly made. Buddhist figures, dragons and plants are carved on each story of the 13.5-meter-high grey marble monument that has stood on the grounds of Kyŏngbokkung since 1960.

The Kyŏngch'ŏnsa Pagoda (left) reveals the mastery of Korea's ancient sculptors.

HYANGWONJŎNG PAVILION

This pavilion, which was constructed by King Kojong in 1868 as a place to stroll and meditate, is lovely any time of year. A favorite subject of artists and photographers, the hexagonal "Pavilion of Far Reaching Fragrance," as its name translates, sits on an island in a lotus pond that is of a very natural design.

The Hyangwonjŏng Pavilion with its surrounding lotus pond (below) is one of the most beautiful sights in Kyŏngbokkung and probably the most famous of the pavilions in Seoul's four palaces.

THE NATIONAL MUSEUM

A complete spectrum of 5,000 years of Korean art can be viewed in the National Museum, which is located at the northern end of Sejongno. Its collection of over 100,000 pieces comprises prehistoric artifacts, excavated tomb ornaments including magnificent gold crowns and girdles, Buddhist sculptures, a number of which weigh several tons, earthenware, stoneware, celadon, porcelain, paintings and ink rubbings. It also has a superb collection of Central Asian art objects and an outstanding collection of Chinese porcelain.

The domed, Renaissance-style building housing the museum dates from the 1920s when it was built to serve two purposes: to house the offices of the Japanese colonial government and to block the view of Kyŏngbokkung Palace. It stands where the southern gate of the palace was located.

This five-story, domed, Renaissance-style building houses the National Museum of Korea in Seoul. Some of Korea's most prized national treasures (opposite: clockwise from top left): gilt-bronze Maitreya Buddha, early 7th century; gold and jade crown from a tomb, 6th century; celadon-glazed, porcelain incense burner, early 12th century; and, white porcelain jar with a bamboo design of underglaze iron, 16th century.

Korea boasts a long history of printing as the world's first movable metal type was invented during Koryŏ. At left is a metal printing plate made during Chosŏn for printing a history book in Chinese. Paintings of the Chosŏn period show a harmonizing of Chinese influences with Korea's own native genius. Some of Chosŏn's most famous painters, both professional and literati, are represented here. Counterclockwise from lower left: Moonlit Landscape, *by Kim Tu-ryang (?–1763);* Orchids, *by Kim Chŏng-hŭi (1786–1856);* Boating Excursion, *by Shin Yun-bok (1758–?);* Plants and Insects, *by Shin Saimdang (1512–59), one of Chosŏn's most famous females; and* Dharma, *by Kim Myŏng-guk (1623-49).*

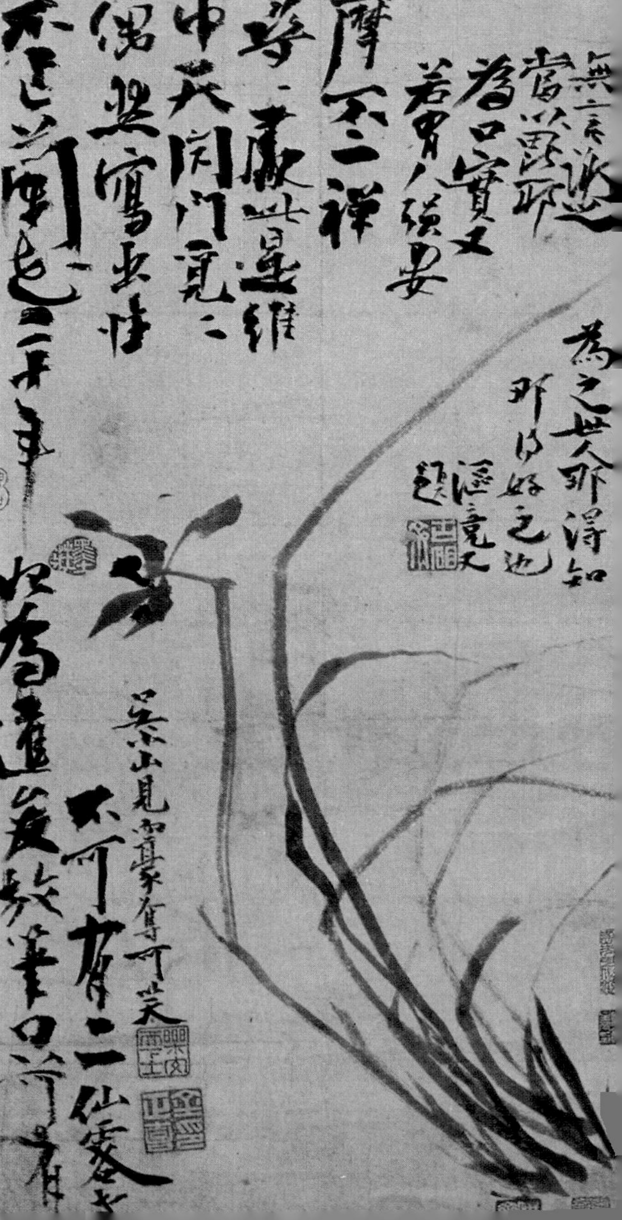

CH'ANGDŎKKUNG

The site of the royal court from the 1590s until the reconstruction of Kyŏngbokkung, Ch'angdŏkkung (Palace of Illustrious Virtue) is the best preserved of all the palaces. It boasts Seoul's oldest original gate Tonhwamun which, having survived the 1592 fires as well as the Korean War, dates from 1412. It is not of the classic square layout like Kyŏngbokkung as it was intended as a detached palace when it was established in 1405 during the reign of Chosŏn's third king T'aejong.

Unlike the other palaces, the 105-acre Ch'angdŏkkung and its garden can only be visited by joining one of the guided tours that are scheduled throughout the day. English, Japanese and, of course, Korean tours are available.

Ch'angdŏkkung's Injŏngjŏn (Hall of Benevolent Government) throne hall, which was first erected in 1405, suffered several fires and was last rebuilt in 1804, is quite similar to Kyŏngbokkung's throne hall. It is surrounded by covered corridors which lead into adjoining reception rooms.

A spectacular screen rich in Confucian symbolism stands behind its elaborate throne. The sun and the moon represent the king's right and left, the mountains represent the "Five Happinesses" and the evergreen pines and the flowing water symbolize long life. A motif of dragons and mythical plants of immortality dominate the intricately carved *yongsang*, as the throne is called, and gilded dragons cavort on the ceiling above it.

Tonhwamun, the entrance to Ch'angdŏkkung Palace.

The carved wooden throne (below) in Injŏngjŏn, the throne hall of Ch'angdŏkkung, stands on a raised dais, under an elaborate canopy, with a colorful screen behind it.

仁政殿

PIWON

In the northeast part of Ch'angdŏkkung is a tranquil woodland which has been called Piwon, or the "Secret Garden," since the Japanese colonial period. First landscaped in 1623, it is an excellent example of the most characteristic features of Korean aesthetics.

Footpaths meander past ponds and streams and over small bridges to reach 28 pavilions and other structures scattered about the garden's 78 acres. The most beautiful of these are the fan-shaped Kwallamjŏng and the ornate, hexagonal Chundŏkjŏng that sit on the edges of Pandoji, a pond shaped like the Korean peninsula. Other interesting structures include a 20-sided pavilion of unusual construction called Puyongjŏng, a house called Yŏn-gyŏngdang where the royal family often went to live like a normal family and a pavilion that inspired many poems written during the Yi Dynasty called Aeryŏnjŏng.

In the southwest corner of Ch'angdŏkkung is a small complex of buildings constructed in 1846 as a housing compound for retired queens. Naksŏnjae, as it is called, is still the residence of descendants of the royal family.

Injŏngjŏn (top left), the throne hall of Ch'angdŏkkung; Hŭijŏngdang (bottom left), a residential building that was moved to Ch'angdŏkkung from Kyŏngbokkung in 1919 to replace the original residence that was destroyed by fire; Puyongjŏng (below), a 20-sided pavilion located in Piwon.

Ŏsumun, or ''Fish Water Gate'' (top), is remarkable for a very heavy tiled roof is supported by two very slender posts. It leads from the Puyongji lotus pond (bottom) up steep steps to a two-story building called Chuhamnu.

Naksŏnjae (Mansion of Joy and Goodness), is the home of the last remaining members of the royal family.

CH'ANGGYŎNGGUNG

The "Palace of Glorious Blessings," Ch'anggyŏnggung stands on the site of a Koryŏ palace that T'aejo used until Kyŏngbokkung was constructed. First built as a detached palace in 1483, it has undergone many reconstructions, the most recent being from 1983 to 1986 to rebuild the structures that were destroyed to make room for a zoo and botanical garden during the Japanese colonial period.

Its throne hall Myŏngjŏngjŏn, which was constructed in 1483, burnt down in 1592 and reconstructed in 1616, is the oldest of the Yi Dynasty throne halls. The hall faces east like the throne halls of Koryŏ palaces instead of south like those of the Yi Dynasty.

Ch'anggyŏnggung not only boasts the oldest throne hall of all the palaces but also a recent facelift as many of its structures which had been destroyed during the colonial period were reconstructed and many of the modern facilities that had been built on its grounds were removed or destroyed.

文政殿

TŎKSUGUNG

Just a few blocks to the west of City Hall and the major hotel district is the palace that was the scene of King Sunjong's abdication of power and the end of the Yi Dynasty era that coincided with Japan's annexation of the country in 1910. It has been called Tŏksugung (Palace of Virtuous Longevity) since 1907 when the name was changed from Kyŏng-un-gung to honor Kojong (r. 1863-1907) who abdicated to his son Sunjong.

First constructed as a villa for a king's grandson in the 15th century, Tŏksugung is now the home of the National Museum of Modern Art Annex. Some ancient scientific inventions, including one of the world's oldest water clocks, can be seen on the palace grounds.

The palatial structures are not representative of the traditional architectural styles of Chosŏn. They date from 1906 when they were built to replace the ones that were destroyed in a 1904 fire that raged out of control for 11 days and destroyed most of the palace.

Tŏksugung (below) is just a few steps from the Seoul Shinmun/Press Center Building, which is visible in the background.
Chunghwajŏn (Hall of Central Harmony), the throne hall of Tŏksugung, is visible through the Chunghwamun Gate (top right). To the northwest of it is Sŏkchojŏn, the home of the National Museum of Modern Art Annex (bottom right).

中和門

CHONGMYO

In the heart of Seoul a stone's throw south of Ch'angdŏkkung is the royal ancestral shrine of the Yi Dynasty Chongmyo. It dates from 1395 when King T'aejo built it for his ancestors' memorial tablets which he had brought from Kaesŏng. The buildings, however, date from 1608 when they were constructed to replace the ones destroyed by Japanese invaders in 1592.

The ancestral tablets of the Yi kings who had direct heirs to the throne, their queens, and their immediate family members are enshrined in the main hall called Chŏngjŏn. Those of the kings who died without heirs and their families are enshrined in a similar building called Yŏngnyŏngjŏn. Ritual vessels and other ceremonial paraphernalia are displayed in some of the other buildings in the walled compound.

Tourists can enter the forested grounds but the Chŏngjŏn and Yŏngnyŏngjŏn halls and their courtyards are only open to the public on the annual ceremonial day, every first Sunday in May. On that day the descendants of the royal Yi family reenact the Confucian-style memorial service with all its pomp and ceremony that was held five times a year during Chosŏn. During the ceremony, brilliantly clad dancers perform to the accompaniment of solemn music played on ancient instruments.

Colorfully costumed musicians play ancient instruments as descendants of the royal Yi family honor their ancestors in Confucian rites (right) at the royal ancestral shrine Chongmyo (below).

GATES

Perhaps the most noticeable of Seoul's ancient monuments are its gates. These tile-roofed structures, which seem to demarcate the downtown area, are colorful reminders of the 17.5-kilometer wall King T'aejo had 198,000 men build around his capital. Of the wall's nine gates, only five remain: Namdaemun and Tongdaemun, the largest and most visible, Ch'angŭimun, Kwanghŭimun and Sukchŏngmun.

Namdaemun (South Gate), which was the main entrance to Seoul during Chosŏn, is located near the Seoul Railroad Station. Built in 1398 and almost completely replaced in 1448, it is the best preserved and most famous of the gates. Its formal name Sungnyemun (Gate of Exalted Ceremony) in Chinese characters can be seen on a plaque underneath its uppermost eaves.

Located near the Seoul Stadium is a smaller gate commonly called Tongdaemun (East Gate). Its real name is Hŭnginjimun (Gate of Uplifting Mercy). The structure dates from 1869 when it was built to replace the original gate that was constructed in 1398. It differs from the others in that it has a semicircular fortifying wall.

Once the southernmost and main entrance to a walled capital, Namdaemun, the South Gate, is now Korea's number one national treasure (below). Tongdaemun, the East Gate, is noted for its semicircular fortifying wall (bottom right). Tongnimmun (top right) is a symbol of Korea's freedom from foreign domination.

TONGNIMMUN

This is a monument erected in 1896 as a symbol of Korea's freedom from foreign domination by the Tongnip Hyŏphoe, a club dedicated to enlightening Koreans to the cause of Korean independence. Independence Arch, as it is generally called in English, is located in Sŏdaemun at the site of Yŏngŭnmun, a gate where annual emissaries from China were greeted from 1539 until almost the end of Chosŏn. Two stone pillars in front of the arch are all that remain of the gate. The arch is one of Korea's first Western-style structures.

KING SEJONG THE GREAT

This bronze statue of King Sejong (r. 1418-50), the fourth king of Chosŏn, has graced the grounds of Tŏksugung since 1968. While his 32-year reign was a time of great scientific achievements and literary development, Sejong is most noted for the invention, by scholars under his direction, of *Han-gŭl*, the Korean phonetic alphabet which enabled Koreans to write in their own language instead of in Chinese.

Han-gŭl is one of the most remarkable writing systems ever devised. The 24-letter alphabet, which follows a rigorous phonological analysis of Korean speech patterns, is also one of the easiest to learn and use. The importance of its invention is celebrated annually on Han-gŭl Day, October 9, with memorial services honoring the great king.

Sejong's other inventions include the *ch'ŭgugi*, a gauge for measuring rainfall that was invented in 1442, some 200 years before such a device was developed in the West; instruments for determining wind direction and velocity; and water clocks.

King Sejong, the inventor of Han-gŭl, *the Korean alphabet, sits in bronze on the grounds of Tŏksugung (below). At the top of the next page is a marble plaque on which an explanation of the alphabet is engraved and at the bottom is a water gauge (left) and a water clock (right) invented during Sejong's reign.*

訓民正音

國之語音異乎中國與文字不相流通故愚民
有所欲言而終不得伸其情者多矣予為此憫
然新制二十八字欲使人人易習便於日用矣
ㄱ 牙音如君字初發聲
並書如虯字初發聲
ㅋ 牙音如快字初發聲
ㆁ 牙音如業字初發聲
ㄷ 舌音如斗字初發聲
並書如覃字初發聲
ㅌ 舌音如呑字初發聲
ㄴ 舌音如那字初發聲
ㅂ 脣音如彆字初發聲
並書如步字初發聲
ㅍ 脣音如漂字初發聲
ㅁ 脣音如彌字初發聲
ㅈ 齒音如即字初發聲
並書如慈字初發聲
ㅊ 齒音如侵字初發聲
ㅅ 齒音如戌字初發聲
並書如邪字初發聲
ㆆ 喉音如挹字初發聲
ㅎ 喉音如虛字初發聲
並書如洪字初發聲
ㅇ 喉音如欲字初發聲
ㄹ 半舌音如閭字初發聲
ㅿ 半齒音如穰字初發聲
ㆍ 如呑字中聲
ㅡ 如即字中聲
ㅣ 如侵字中聲
ㅗ 如洪字中聲
ㅏ 如覃字中聲
ㅜ 如君字中聲
ㅓ 如業字中聲
ㅛ 如欲字中聲
ㅑ 如穰字中聲
ㅠ 如戌字中聲
ㅕ 如彆字中聲
終聲復用初聲ㅇ連書脣音之下則為脣輕音
初聲合用則並書終聲同ㆍㅡㅗㅜㅛㅠ附書
初聲之下ㅣㅏㅓㅑㅕ附書於右凡字必合而
成音左加一點則去聲二則上聲無則平聲入
聲加點同而促急

PAGODA PARK

On Chongno Street, just a couple of blocks from City Hall and the hotel district, is Pagoda Park, once the site of a Buddhist temple called Won-gaksa. The recently renovated park is so-called because of a beautiful 15th-century, 10-story pagoda that graces its grounds. The pagoda resembles the 10-story Koryŏ pagoda of Kyŏngch'ŏnsa Temple which stands on the grounds of Kyŏngbok-kung. It is one of only a few relics that were left when the temple was dismantled in 1515.

However, it is for its connection with the independence movement that Pagoda Park is most famous. A ceremony is held here every March 1 to commemorate the March 1, 1919 public reading of the Korean Declaration of Independence which touched off nationwide demonstrations protesting Japanese colonial rule.

Ten large bronze bas-reliefs depicting some events related to the independence movement are located throughout the park. The Declaration of Independence and the names of its signers can be seen on a stone monument. The park is a favorite gathering place for senior citizens and thus a good place to see people clad in traditional clothes.

Samilmun Gate (below), the entrance to Pagoda Park. At right (clockwise from top left), a bas-relief describing the March 1, 1919 public reading of the Korean Declaration of Independence from Japan; a statue of Son Pyŏng-hŭi, the leader of the Samil Independence Movement; and ancient stele on which information about Won-gaksa Temple is inscribed; and, the Won-gaksa Pagoda.

POSHIN-GAK

Located at the Chongno intersection is a two-story belfry called Poshin-gak. Chongno actually means "Bell Street" and is where King T'aejo had a bell for signaling the opening and closing of the city gates hung in 1395 as, at that time, it was the approximate center of the city.

However, the bell that hangs in today's belfry, which was remodeled in 1985, is not T'aejo's bell but a recently cast one; T'aeio's disappeared in the 1592 fires that ravaged the city. The one it replaced, which was cast in 1468 and originally hung at Won-gaksa Temple, is now displayed in the National Museum.

Like all large Korean bells, the one in Poshin-gak is rung by striking its side with a large log suspended from the roof of the belfry. It is struck 33 times at midnight on New Year's Eve to ring in the New Year.

At a major intersection in central Seoul is this traditional-style, two story bell pavilion called Poshin-gak.

These shots of the Hotel Shilla, the Lotte Hotel and the Seoul Plaza Hotel show what a mosaic of old and new Seoul is.

MT. NAMSAN

Rising up in the middle of Seoul's forest of concrete, steel and glass is a mountain called Namsan. Though its lower slopes have been eaten away by commercial and residential areas, it still offers Seoulites a convenient retreat from the hustle and bustle of the city and a chance to enjoy nature. It has been developed as a park since 1910 and is officially called Namsan Municipal Park.

The summit is 265 meters above sea level. It can be reached by a winding two-lane road or by cable car. Atop the peak is an octagonal pavilion and the Seoul Tower, a 236.7-meter-high telecommunications tower that is the Orient's highest above sea level. A revolving observation deck with dining facilities is located at the top of the tower.

A city library, an arboretum, the National Theater and a number of other cultural facilities as well as several major hotels are located on the slopes of Mt. Namsan. The slopes are also dotted with statues of historical figures.

The eight-sided P'algakchŏng pavilion atop Mt. Namsan (below) and the mountain's crowning finial, the Seoul Tower (right). The two offer a 360-degree panoramic view of Seoul.

TRANSPORTATION

Buses, subways and metered taxis comprise Seoul's major primary public transportation systems, with only taxis operating around the clock. They are all fairly cheap and quite efficient.

Buses presently carry the majority of people but, with the recent expansion of the subway system to link the major suburbs with the center of the city, more and more people are expected to become subway users. The four subway lines have a total length of 116.5 kilometers and are capable of transporting over 3 million passengers a day. Their stops are well marked and conveniently located near the major business and shopping districts, schools and universities, transportation centers and sports complexes as well as many of the palaces and other places of interest.

Express trains and buses link Seoul with other towns and cities throughout the nation as well as with major beach and mountain resorts and other tourist attractions. Airline service is also available to some of the major cities and resorts. Seoul is connected with just about every major capital in the world via direct flights or with connecting flights at major international airports in the Far East.

Trains to almost any part of the country can be taken from the Seoul Railroad Station (below). The station, which dates from the early 1920's, is rather centrally located and can be easily reached by taxi, bus or subway, the major means of public transportation.

67

4200

THE MODERN CITY

A microcosm of the whole nation and its long colorful history, today's Seoul is truly the "center of everything." The office of the President as well as the National Assembly and the Supreme Court are located in Seoul. All the government ministries and the head offices of national and private industries are located in Seoul and its satellite cities.

Banks, economic organizations, the top universities and colleges, research institutes, libraries, cultural facilities, museums, theaters, sports complexes and amusement parks abound in Seoul. It is also where the radio and television networks as well as the publishers of the major newspapers and magazines are concentrated.

Seoul is one of the world's most vibrant metropolises and its residents are enjoying a new age or pride and prosperity.

The granite National Assembly Building (below) is located on Yŏŭido, an island of reclaimed land in the middle of the Han River.
The convergence of six streets makes the intersection in front of City Hall (top right) one of the busiest in Seoul.
Once visible from great distances, the Namdaemun Gate (bottom right) is now dwarfed by the offices of some of Korea's major business conglomerates.

This panoramic view of Seoul (top) from a hill behind Tŏksugung Palace shows what a harmonious blending of the old and the new Seoul is. At bottom left is a luxurious housing area in northern Seoul as

seen from a hotel and at bottom right is a more populated residential area on the southwestern slopes of Mt. Namsan.

CONSTRUCTION

Seoul is enjoying a construction boom as evidenced by ever-present cranes that seem to be reaching for the sky and the dawn-to-dusk din made by jackhammers, bulldozers and other earth-moving equipment, not to mention its constantly changing skyline. A frenzy of construction in the downtown is producing dozens of huge skyscrapers to meet the needs of Seoul's expanding business activities while housing complexes and recreational facilities are springing up, seemingly overnight, in the area south of the Han River.

This building boom is due in part to a new age of affluence spawned by a rapidly increasing standard of living.

The area that has been most visibly affected by the boom is Yŏŭido, an island of reclaimed land in the middle of the Han River. It is known as Seoul's "Little Manhattan" because of its soaring office buildings, expensive apartment blocks and chic nightlife, not to mention it is the site of the stock exchange. The Yŏng-dong area has also been greatly affected. It is commonly referred to as the "New Myŏng-dong" because of its concentration of exclusive shops, expensive restaurants and entertainment facilities. Some department stores and amusement parks such as Lotte World have recently been constructed there.

The side streets along Chongno, one of Seoul's busiest thoroughtares, is a favorite meeting place for young people due to its great concentration of teahouses, bars, bakeries, Western fast-food chains, gamerooms and the like(below). This street separating the major hotel district and the Myŏng-dong shopping district is lined with banks and department stores(top right). By the artificial lake of Sŏk ch'on, Lotte World itself satisfies all the requisites to city life with the hotel, the department store, and Lotte Adventure amusement park(bottom right).

TE WORLD

CHRISTIANITY

Seoul's skyline is punctuated by many large churches and cathedrals. In fact, there are some 3,820 in the metropolis, several of which offer multilingual services. The more than 400,000-member Yoido Full Gospel Church (*Sunbogŭm Kyohoe*) is the largest in the world. It is symbolic of the unprecedented rate at which Christianity has grown since its introduction to Korea a little over 200 years ago.

Catholicism, which celebrated its bicentennial in 1984, claims more than 1.6 million believers, while Protestantism, which observed its centennial in 1982, claims more than 5.3 million. However, Christianity has a greater influence than these figures indicate, due in part to the great emphasis it puts on education.

Korea's oldest Catholic church, the Gothic-style, red brick Myŏng-dong Cathedral in Seoul's fashionable Myŏng-dong shopping district opened its doors in 1898.
At right (clockwise from top left): a Sunday service in the Yoido Full Gospel Church, the world's largest church; the Seoul Foreigners' Cemetery where many of the first missionaries to Korea are buried; and, a statue of Father Andrew Kim Tae-gŏn, Korea's first ordained priest who was made a saint in 1984, on the grounds of Chŏltusan, a shrine to Christian martyrs overlooking the Han River which is located near the Yanghwadaegyo Bridge.

BELIEVE

BUDDHISM

With approximately 7.5 million believers, Buddhism, which came to Korea via China in 372 A.D. and so flourished that the country was called the "Land of Pagodas," has the greatest following of Korea's more than 250 religious sects. It is so strong that Buddha's birthday, which varies from year to year as it is April 8th of the lunar calendar, was made a national holiday in 1975.

In Seoul alone, where the religion claims the least followers, there are more than 1,570 temples. Chogyesa, which is located in Anguk-dong not far from Kyŏngbokkung, Ch'angdŏkkung and Pagoda Park, is one of the more interesting. Founded in 1910, it is now the headquarters of the Chogye sect, which is the nation's largest Buddhist sect. It hums with activity, especially on Buddha's birthday when it is the site of a colorful lantern parade.

Lanterns and prayers are central to the celebrations on Buddha's Birthday. All day monks pray for those whose names are written on the tags that dangle from the paper lanterns that make rainbows of the temple grounds and at night each worshiper-owner of a lantern lights a candle in it to pray for Buddha's blessing.

불기2529년
봉축
오신날

오부불회
강봉호

CONFUCIANISM

While officially it claims only around 800,000 followers, Confucianism thrives more in Korea than in any other nation as it greatly influences the outlook and actions of all the people. It is not exactly a religion and it is more than a philosophy—it is a way of life. Its basic values, including deference to age, respect for those superior and responsibility to family and friends first, are well-practiced ideals which have only been slightly modified in recent times.

The tradition of Confucianism in Korea goes back long before the introduction of Buddhism in 372 A.D., but it was not until the establishment of Chosŏn that it enjoyed a golden age. The most tangible proof of its existence is the more than 250 shrines to Confucius and his Chinese and Korean disciples that are scattered throughout the country. The largest is on the grounds of Seoul's Sungkyun-gwan University which, established in 1288, is Korea's oldest university as well as its center of Confucianism. Every spring and fall it is the site of colorful memorial services honoring the spirit of Confucius.

Myŏngnyundang, which is a part of the Sŏnggyun-gwan Shrine, is a lecture hall where Confucian classics were taught during the Chosŏn period. Ancient music, dance and colorful costumes are an integral part of the Sŏkchŏn *memorial ceremonies that are held at the shrine every spring and fall (right).*

八佾舞

CULTURE AND ARTS

Seoul's cultural scene is a blending of much that is traditional with influences from the West. Artistic activity is brisk as is apparent in the abundance of galleries and museums. Performances of all types of music, dance and theater arts, both Korean and Western, are frequent. The city boasts two well-established opera companies, two full-scale orchestras, not to mention the Palace Orchestra that dates to the 15th century, and a ballet company as well as dozens of small dance companies, theater groups and choirs.

The Sejong Cultural Center, about a fiveminute walk from City Hall Plaza, offers a wide variety of musical and theatrical performances by Korean as well as foreign artists and is the site of many international festivals, conferences and other events. The National Theater, on the eastern slope of Mt. Namsan, is noted for its traditional Korean music and folk arts performances, while the Seoul Arts Center in Sŏch'o-dong, its contemporary ones.

Of special note is the Korean Culture and Arts Foundation in Tongsung-dong. In front of it is a street lined with cafes, coffeehouses, galleries and stamp shops called Taehangno. On weekends the street is transformed into a mall where local artists and craftsmen display their works and dances and concerts

Performances of folk and mask dances can be enjoyed at the Seoul Nori Madang, an open-air stage beside the Sŏkch'on Lake near the Seoul Sports Complex.

The Sejong Cultural Center (left), can seat 4,200 persons in its main auditorium which has a stage that can accommodate 500 performers at one time. It is the scene of many plays and concerts by Korean as well as Western artists (top). Traditional performances like this colorful court dance (bottom) are generally staged in the National Theater.

KOREAN DANCE

Dance, along with music, is by far one of the most highly developed of the performing arts in Korea. Court and folk are the two main types of traditional dance. The first, comprising the dances done at the Sŏnggyun-gwan shrine to Confucius and the royal ancestral shrine Chongmyo and those performed as entertainment for the king and his court, is characterized by dignity and grace, while the latter, improvised by farmers during planting and harvest times, is characterized by acrobatic vigor.

Korean dance is a unique blend of poetry, music and rhythmical steps and motions. In and of itself it only strives to convey a mood, but stories are often communicated verbally or through acting.

Many of the court and folk dances have been designated "intangible cultural treasures" to ensure their survival. However, most of the traditional dance performances seen on today's stages, particularly those seen on television and in dinner theaters, are modern adaptations. The National Theater's National Classical Music Institute, which is dedicated to the preservation of Korea's traditional music and dance, offers the most authentic performances.

Korean dances (counterclockwise from below): Pukch'um *(Drum Dance); the highly popular* Puch'aech'um *(Fan Dance);* Changgoch'um *(Hourglass Drum Dance); and* Sŭngmu *(Monk's Dance).*

HOUSING

Traditional Korean houses are generally a tile-roofed, one-story, L-or U-shaped structure made of wood and clay comprising several rooms.

The corners of the roofs are tilted slightly upward giving the houses a smiling appearance. The floors are *ondol*; that is, they are heated via a system of under-the-floor flues that carry warm air from a central source of heat. The system well augments the Korean lifestyle as Koreans have traditionally sat and slept on cushions and mats on the floor.

Large brick houses of several stories and high-rise apartment complexes are rapidly replacing traditional Korean-type housing. With these changes, Western-style furnishings including dining tables and chairs, sofas and coffee tables are increasingly replacing the low tables, chests and cushions traditionally used in Korean homes. However, there is one traditional feature that is maintained in even the most modern houses and apartments—*ondol* floors. The *ondol* system is generally used for bedrooms and steam heat for the rest of the home.

Traditional tile-roofed houses are rapidly giving way to houses of several stories and high-rise apartments, which has prompted the Seoul city government to designate some residential areas for the construction of only traditional-style structures.

COLLEGES AND UNIVERSITIES

Of Korea's 107 colleges and universities, 34 are located in Seoul. There are also 15 junior colleges and five three-year nursing colleges in the city. Some of them are nestled amongst the skyscrapers of the downtown area while some are located in the rolling hills of the city's outskirts.

Seoul National University, Yonsei University, Korea University (Koryŏ) and Ewha Womans University, all located in Seoul, are considered the nation's most prestigious universities. With an enrollment of almost 30,000 Seoul National is the largest.

Many of the colleges and universities have very fine museums that are open to the public. Some of the most unusual ones include Dankook University's Suk Joo-sun Memorial Museum of Korean Folk Art which displays mostly traditional clothes and accessories, Soongsil University's Korean Christian Museum which exhibits items related to missionary work in Korea, the King Sejong University Museum which displays traditional clothing, furniture and ornaments, and Kyunghee University's Natural History Museum, which is the first of its kind in Asia.

The campuses of Seoul National University (below), which is located on the slopes of Mt. Kwanaksan to the south of Seoul, and Kyunghee University (bottom right), which is located in the northeastern part of Seoul, are two of the most beautiful campuses in the city.
College students take great interest in Korea's traditional performing arts as these scenes at the Taehakno ''Street of Culture'' well illustrate (top right).

8.14 전국
마로니에
8.15-20
선각자여
이호영·정
8.22-27
검은새
정복근작/
8.29-9.3

LEISURE

As Korea is a peninsular country of mountains and rivers, hiking and fishing are two of the most popular pastimes. Outdoor enthusiasts can enjoy mountaineering, rock climbing, and hunting. Golf, tennis, bowling, archery, water and snow skiing, skating, sailing swimming, skin diving, windsurfing and ice sailing are available for sports lovers.

There are 16 golf courses in the Seoul vicinity, all within an hour's drive of the downtown. As for swimming, the major sports complexes have pools open to the public as do many of the first-class hotels. Snow skiing is available at the Dragon Valley, Yongin, Chŏnmasan, Alps and Bears resorts, all of which are easily accessible, while horse racing can be enjoyed at the Ttuksŏm Track in Seoul's southeastern suburbs. The gambler can find his game in any number of hotel casinos.

The Children's Grand Park, the Seoul Grand Park and the Yongin Family Land have something to please children of all ages—rides, games, fun houses, zoos, animal shows, gardens and plenty of picnic areas.

The Children's Grand Park (left) and the Seoul Grand Park (bottom right) are conveniently located amusement centers that have plenty to attract both young and old alike. The latter's porpoise show and zoo are especially popular (top right).

KOREAN FOOD

Diverse. Spicy. Earthy. Cool. Colorful. Korean food is an experience, with dishes sharing no resemblance to those of any other country. While dishes range from the bland to the peppery hot, most carry the blended tang and aroma of garlic, red pepper, leeks, soy sauce, and sesame seed and oil.

Rice, either plain or cooked with other grains such as barley and millet and/or a variety of beans, is the main dish. *Kimch'i*, a pungent, fermented dish generally comprising cabbage, turnip or cucumbers seasoned with salt, garlic, onions, ginger, red pepper and shellfish, is the next most important component of a Korean meal and Korea's most famous food. It titillates the tongue as well as supplies Vitamin C.

Soup, or *kuk*, is also a vital part of every meal. Spicy or bland, it generally contains meat, fish or seaweed. Thick soups made of soybean paste and soybean curd are especially popular. Rounding out the meal are what is called *panch'an*, or side dishes. These generally include parboiled vegetables, herbs and roots that are lightly seasoned with sesame oil, garlic, soy sauce and ground and toasted sesame seeds. A seafood or meat dish is often included.

There are, of course, holiday foods as well as special dishes that are a must for important occasions and celebrations. These include *ttŏk*, rice cakes dusted with roasted soy, barley or millet or embellished with aromatic mugwort leaves.

The Korea House (opposite) is an excellent example of traditional architecture and the perfect place to get a taste of Korean cuisine and culture. Shinsŏllo, *or ''Angel's Brazier'', and* pulgogi, *grilled seasoned meat, are two of the most popular dishes for special occasions, while* kimch'i *is a must at every meal (counterclokwise from top left).*

As the Sŏl sang, or New Year's table(bottom), shows a Korean meal is fit for a king; and indeed, some of today's special dishes were prepared for only royalty in times past. Special dinners and holiday feasts may consist of as many as 15 dishes, but most meals consist of five or six. Some favorite foods are

(clockwise from opposite top left): kalbi, *or grilled beef ribs;* ttŏk, *or rice cakes; steamed red snapper and prawns;* chŏn-gol, *sliced meat and vegetables simmered in a seasoned broth; and, of course,* kimch'i *which requires much time and effort to prepare.*

LIFESTYLE

Much of Korea's traditional way of life is on the wane but many of its customs and traditions are still very much alive and many aspects of Korean social consciousness such as respect for one's parents, deference to superiors, the role of the eldest son and trust between friends are still preserved in time-honored fashions. Korean family life remains close-knit, not only between parents and children, but also between brothers and sisters and their spouses. While there is an increasing tendency towards nuclear families, the extended family is still most common and the housewife spends most of her time at home.

A young couple enjoy an elaborate dinner with their family in a traditional-style restaurant (below). At right (clockwise from top left), a traditionally clad woman employs the same methods her ancestors did to ''iron'' a piece of bedding material; some women hand-sew a hanbok, *or Korean dress; and some women practice calligraphy.*

FUN AND GAMES

Traditional games are still popular as they were centuries ago. And some of them are an integral part of traditional celebrations.

Among the most popular is *yut*, a game derived from ancient divination rituals that is similar to backgammon. The object of the game is to be the first to move four "men" all the way around a square diagram of 20 dots. Moves are determined by a toss of the *yut* sticks, which are flat on one side and convex on the other. The game is traditionally played on New Year's Day.

Nŏlttwigi, a jumping game similar to seesawing, is popular among girls, especially on Tano, a spring festival day determined by the lunar calendar. The popularity it enjoyed in olden days is said to have stemmed directly from the fact that women were not allowed outside the premises of their homes; it allowed them to see up and over the walls of their compounds.

Another popular folk game is *yŏn nalligi*, or kite flying. It is traditionally most ardently pursued around the time of the first full moon of the lunar year.

Traditionally clad children enjoy nŏlttwigi *(lower left) and* yut *(right), two games commonly played on traditional holidays, while a farmer's band performs in front of a reproduction of a traditional upper-class residence (below).*

The traditional performing arts, like this mask dance (left) and mask drama (below), are enjoying a revival.
At right, a bridegroom is traveling to his bride's home in a reenactment of a traditional wedding custom that is no longer practiced.

IMPORTANT EVENTS

The most important events in the life of a Korean are the *paek il*, or 100th day after birth, the *tol*, or first birthday, and the *hwan-gap*, or 60th birthday. *Paek il*, which is only celebrated if the child is healthy at the time, is observed with a small feast for friends and family. *Tol* is a ritual through which the future of the child is indicated.

The 60th birthday is especially important, for it marks the completion of a full cycle of the Oriental zodiac, a great accomplishment before the advent of modern medicine. It is a time for great feasting and merrymaking.

Marriage, of course, is also an important event. The marriage ceremony itself has changed greatly but many of the traditional practices, including matchmaking, and ceremonies leading to it are still followed, although much modified for today's lifestyles. Most weddings are now held in public wedding halls with the bride dressed in a Western-style lace gown and the groom in a dark suit. However, traditional Korean weddings are becoming increasingly popular.

A traditional Korean wedding (left and bottom left) is a very colorful affair involving many rituals rich in symbolism. At bottom right, a one-year-old sits before a birthday feast to predict his future. At right, a coffin is carried to a burial site in the enactment of a traditional funeral at the Korean Folk Village, where many traditional events and ceremonies can be observed.

SHAMANISM

It is not unusual for a well-to-do family to consult a fortuneteller prior to setting a wedding day, selecting a day to move or choosing a name for a newborn child. Nor is it uncommon for a highly educated businessman, when he moves into a new building, to hold a party at which a ritualistic offering of food and wine is made to pray for the success of his business. While they may not be aware of it, they are going through rituals inspired by Shamanism, the belief that the visible world is pervaded by invisible forces or spirits that affect the daily lives of the living.

Central to Shamanism is the *mudang*, or shaman, whose primary role is to perform a *kut*, or exorcising ceremony, by which she can enter the spirit world and render the destructive power of a spirit harmless. Other important functions of the *mudang* include curing disease and afflictions and telling fortunes.

A shaman dances, entertaining a spirit in front of an offering(below). Kut, Korean Shamanist rituals, are central to a mudang's fascinating dances. Today, the rituals are held mostly for the purpose of preserving the traditional cultures(top right). A fortuneteller reads a man's fortune and offers advice (bottom right).

SPORTS

Koreans have traditionally been lovers of physical exercise and sportsmanship as murals discovered in ancient tombs have shown. Korea's athletes have performed well in international competitions. They won 33 medals—twelve gold, ten silver, eleven bronze—from the 1988 Seoul Summer Olympics to rank 4th in the world.

Koreans are especially enthusiastic about spectator sports, particularly soccer, baseball, boxing, volleyball and basketball, and are rightfully proud of *t'aekwondo* and *ssirŭm* wrestling, two sports indigenous to Korea.

The World T'aekwondo Federation(WTF), with its headquarters in Seoul, was officially approved as the controlling body of the sport by the International Olympic Committee in 1980. T'aekwondo was a demonstration sport in the 1988 Seoul Olympics.

The Ministry of Sports was established in 1982 to promote physical education and sports throughout the country and provide the necessary government assistance for the successful staging of the 1986 Asian Games and the 1988 Summer Olympics.

The Games of the 24th Olympiad were

successfully concluded after a 16-day run in Seoul from September 17 to October 2, 1988. The monumental success of the Seoul Games was the result of the all-out efforts Koreans made.

Partly as a result of the 1988 Seoul Olympics, Korea has many world-class sports facilities. Located just south of the Han River, the Seoul Sports Complex includes the Olympic Stadium with a seating capacity of 75,000, two gymnasiums for basketball and boxing, an indoor swimming pool, a baseball park and a warm-up field. It is less than half an hour drive from the center of Seoul and 45 minutes from the Kimpo International Airport. Four kilometers from it is the Olympic Park comprising a velodrome, three gymnasiums, an indoor swimming pool, and tennis courts.

The Han River Regatta for canoeing and rowing and the Seoul Equestrian Park also represent the finest standard of Korea's sports facilities comprising the T'aenŭng Athletes Village where advanced athletic training techniques are studied.

A bird's-eye view of the Seoul Sports Complex which was the main venue of the 1988 Summer Olympics.

Koreans are showing increased interest in their own native sports of ssirŭm *wrestling (left) and* t'aekwondo *(below) as well as in international favorites like marathon racing. Seoul hosts an international marathon every spring (bottom).*
The Olympic Stadium which was the site of the opening and closing ceremonies and other main events of the 1986 Asian Games (top right) and the 1988 Summer Olympics (bottom right), can accomodate 100,000 spectators.

제 10 회 아시아경기대회
10th ASIAN GAMES SEOUL 1986
GoldStar VIDEO TAPE

IT'AEWON

Once a way station for travelers on their way to the ancient capital, It'aewon is now a growing mecca for bargain hunters. The main thoroughfare of the "Garden of Peaceful Pear Blossoms" extends some 1.5 kilometers from the east edge of the American military garrison Yongsan all the way to the Hannam-dong Rotary. It is lined on both sides with hundreds of shops and arcades selling ready-made sports clothes; all types of athletic shoes; sweaters; silk dresses; jeans and slacks; tailor-made suits, coats, shirts and dresses; made-to-order shoes and boots; eel skin purses, belts, shoes, wallets and attache cases; and, luggage in all shapes and sizes. There are also shops specializing in antiques, brassware and jewelry as well as gift items. There is also a shop of the world-famous Jindo Fur Salon where non-residents of Korea can purchase furs at great savings.

But It'aewon is more than a shopper's paradise, it is also an entertainment spot that boasts well over 200 restaurants, bars and clubs that offer a healthy sampling of the latest in popular, jazz, disco and country-western music. It is also the home of many

Shop after shop of bargains line It'aewon's major thoroughfare. The area caters to foreign shoppers as evidenced in the abundance of English signboards.

well-known fast-food chains that serve pizza, chicken, hamburgers, donuts and the like.

English is widely spoken amongst It'aewon's shopkeepers and purchases can be made with American dollars. The area is about a 10-minute taxi ride or a 20-minute bus ride from the downtown area.

Native crafts and products such as ceramics, lacquerware and mother-of-pearl, brassware, bamboo products, baskets, jewelry, and ginseng are to be found in all department stores, underground arcades,

hotel gift shops and stores catering to tourists.

INSA-DONG

Along a narrow street in Insa-dong that foreigners call "Mary's Alley" is Seoul's time-honored antique and curio district. Both sides of the street that extends from near Pagoda Park to the Anguk-dong Rotary, as well many of its side alleys, are lined with shops offering pottery and ceramics from Korea's earliest kingdoms not to mention paintings, calligraphy, sculptures, ancient jewelry, books and furniture and other household paraphernalia.

There are also numerous shops specializing in reproductions of traditional ceramics and Chosŏn-period furniture. There are also many shops selling beautiful Korean-style bedding and cushions and a good number of art galleries and excellent restaurants in the area.

Shoppers should be aware that antiques are subject to a government regulation that stipulates that items that are of great historic or cultural value can not be taken out of the country.

"Mary's Alley," with its innumerable shops of all shapes and sizes, some even on wheels, is one of Seoul's most interesting areas to shop or just browse.

다방
OB베어

용운당
이발
못
畫廊
光山畫廊

Jewelry, curios, books and art objects of today as well as bygone eras can be found in Insa-dong's ''Mary's Alley.''

TRADITIONAL MARKETS

One of the best places in Seoul to experience the true hustle-bustle of a traditional marketplace is the Namdaemun Market which is near the gate for which it is named. It is a maze of overcrowded streets and alleys overflowing with fruits and vegetables, clothes, pottery, baskets and merchants hawking their wares and men and women haggling over prices.

The Tongdaemun Market, which also takes its name from the gate it is near, is much larger and offers a wide variety of products ranging from foodstuff to textiles to machine parts. It comprises about a dozen block-long, two- and three-story buildings as well as endless rows of open stalls. It is well known as Korea's silk center but it also has a great selection of cottons, wools and other fabrics at very affordable prices.

Smaller versions of these markets can be found in almost every large housing area. And all of them can be fun to browse through.

As these pictures show, almost every imaginable commodity—clothes, tubing, ceramics, ginseng, chicken, pots and pans, the list goes on and on—can be found in the streets and alleys of Seoul's traditional markets.

대도상가
대동정육점

Shopping in the Namdaemun and Tongdaemun markets can be both fun and easy as the merchandise tends to be segregated with shops dealing in the same kind of goods grouped together: silks dominate

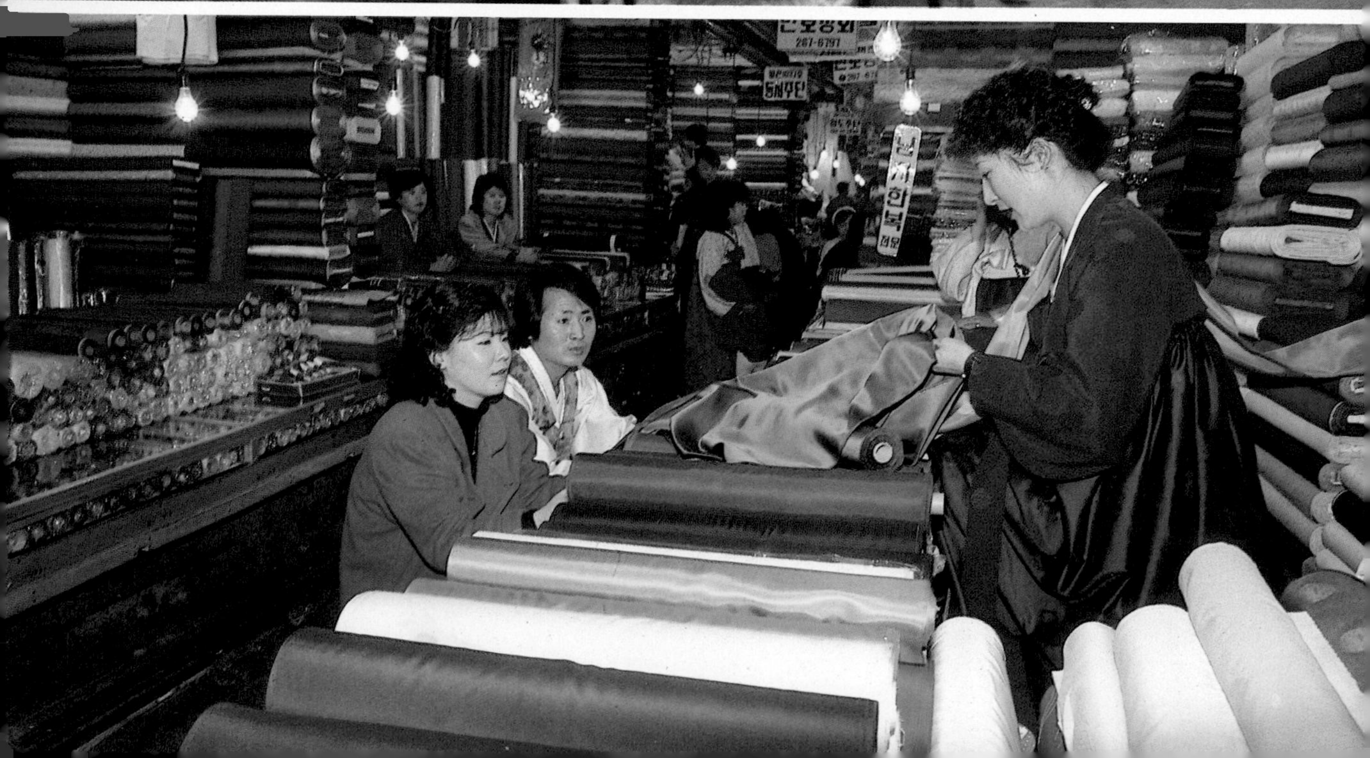

one area, clothes another, and so on and so forth. The markets also have their own special fast foods such as vegetable pancakes, laver-wrapped rice, sausage and sliced pork.

라이프

The 63-story Daehan Life Insurance Building on Youido Island is one of the tallest buildings in Asia. It is commonly referred to as "DLI-63".

Basic Korean Conversation

● Greetings

안녕하세요 ? Annyŏnghaseyo ?	Good morning.
네, 안녕하세요 ? Ne, annyŏnghaseyo ?	Good morning.
반갑습니다. Pangapssŭmnida.	Pleased to meet you.
또 뵙겠어요. Tto poepkessŏyo.	See you again.
안녕히 가세요. Annyŏnghi kaseyo.	Good bye.(said to the person leaving)
안녕히 계세요. Annyŏnghi keseyo.	Good bye.(said to the preson staying as you leave)
어떠십니까 ? Ŏttŏshimnikka ?	How are you ?
요즘 바쁘십니까 ? Yojŭm pappŭshimnikka ?	Are you busy lately ?
좋습니다. 감사합니다. Chossŭmnida. Kamsahamnida.	Fine. Thank you.
안녕히 주무십시오. Annyŏnghi chumushipshio.	Good night.

● Introduction

성함이 무엇이죠 ? Sŏnghami muŏshijyo ?	What's your name, please ?
제 이름은 이명호입니다. Che irŭmŭn Imyŏnghoimnida.	My name is Yi Myong-ho.
또 만날 수 있길 바랍니다. Tto mannal su itkil paramnida.	I hope we can meet again sometime.
잘 부탁 드립니다. Chal put'ak tŭrimnida.	Do me a favor.